UNOFFICIAL
KANYE WEST
TWEET COLORING BOOK

Copyright © 2021 Lemon Tree Coloring

Lemon Tree Coloring is an imprint of Polygon Publishing LTD.

www.polygonpublishing.com

ISBN-13: 978-1-914117-06-0

This book is not authorized, endorsed by or affiliated with Kanye West.

THIS BOOK BELONGS TO

....

....

....

TEST YOUR COLORS HERE!

Use this page to compare colors and shades.

We have put in a lot of effort to prevent any color bleed through the pages (hence the black reverse pages). However, color bleeding may still occur. **Our Tip:** Slip a piece of paper or cardboard behind the page you are coloring in, to avoid casting hue to the next page. **HAPPY COLORING!**

TEST YOUR COLORS HERE!

Use this page to compare colors and shades.

We have put in a lot of effort to prevent any color bleed through the pages (hence the black reverse pages). However, color bleeding may still occur. **Our Tip:** Slip a piece of paper or cardboard behind the page you are coloring in, to avoid casting hue to the next page. **HAPPY COLORING!**

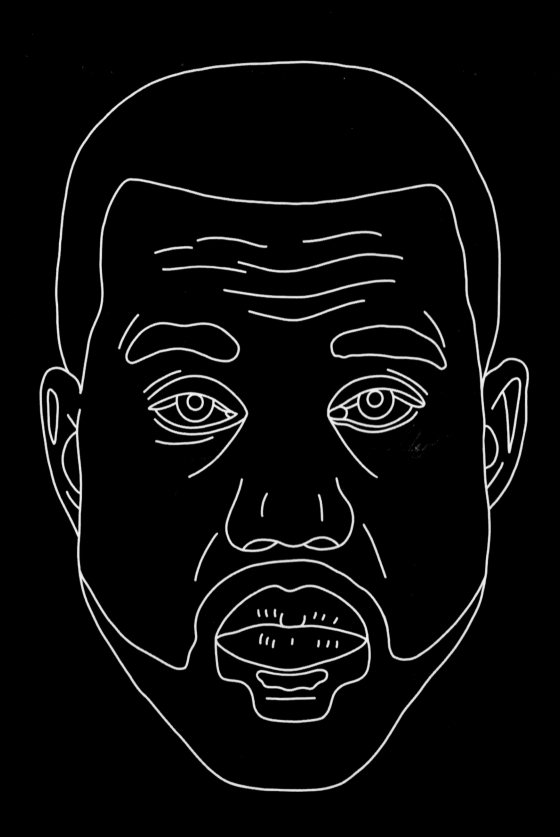

@kanyewest

I no longer have a manager.
I can't be managed.

Retweets and comments   Likes

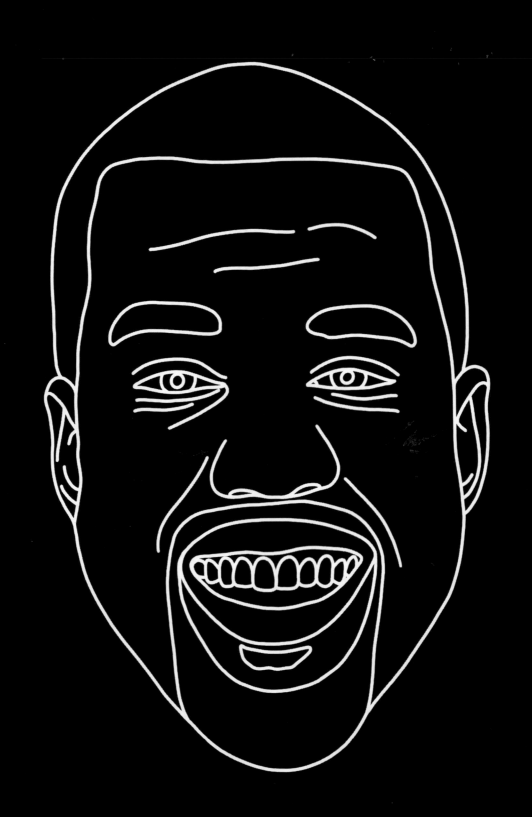

 @kanyewest

Super inspired by my visit to Ikea today, really amazing company... my mind is racing with the possibilities...

Retweets and comments   Likes

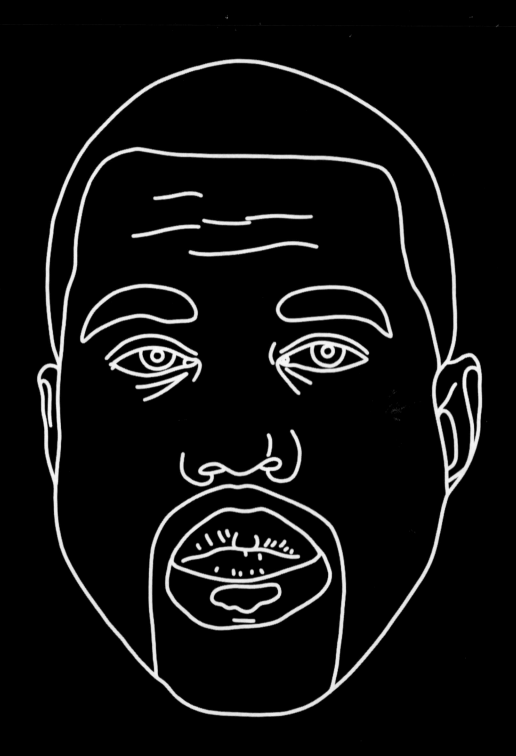

@kanyewest

not smiling makes me smile

Retweets and comments   Likes

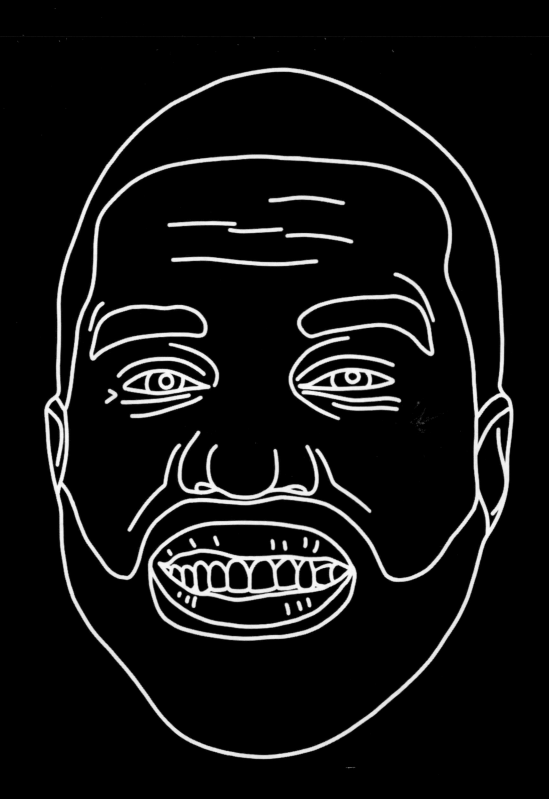

Sometimes I push the door close button on people running towards the elevator. I just need my own elevator sometimes. My sanctuary.

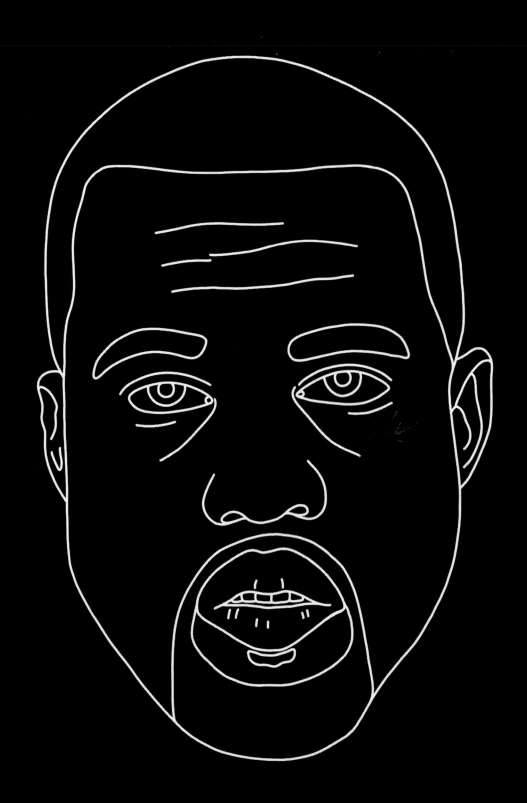

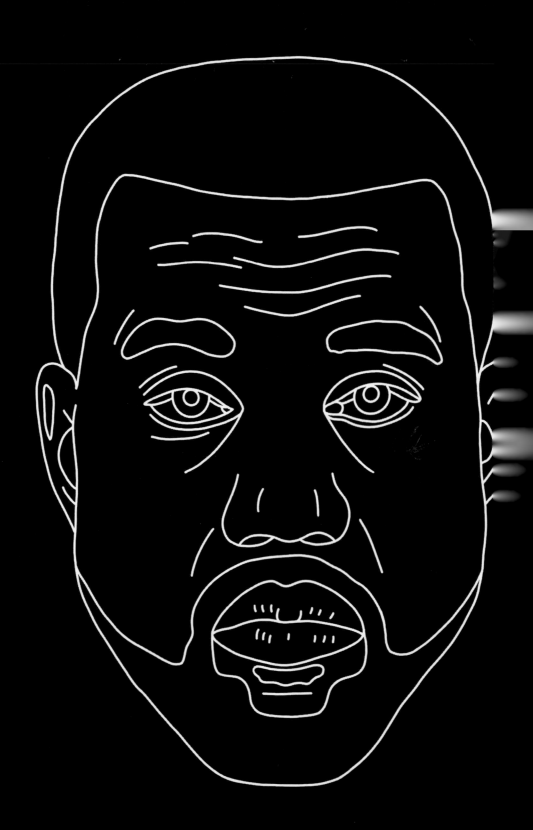

 @kanyewest

Sometimes I get emotional over fonts

Retweets and comments   Likes

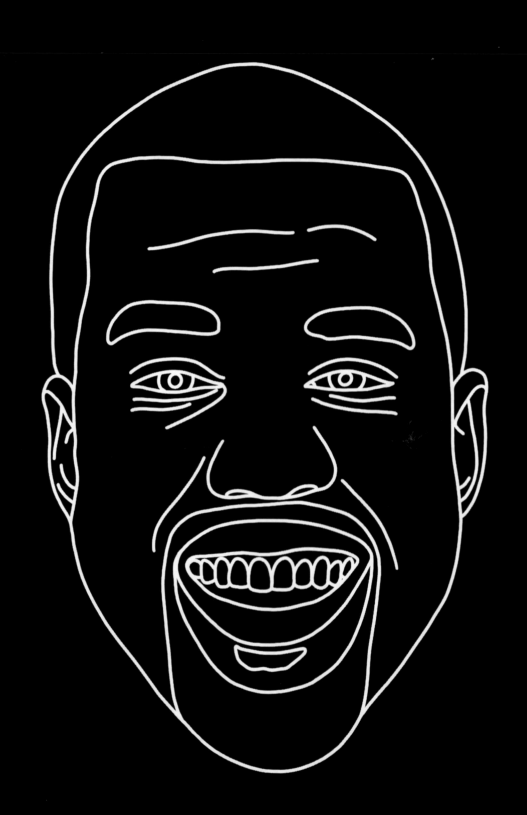

Have you ever thought you were in love with someone but then realized you were staring in a mirror for 20 minutes?

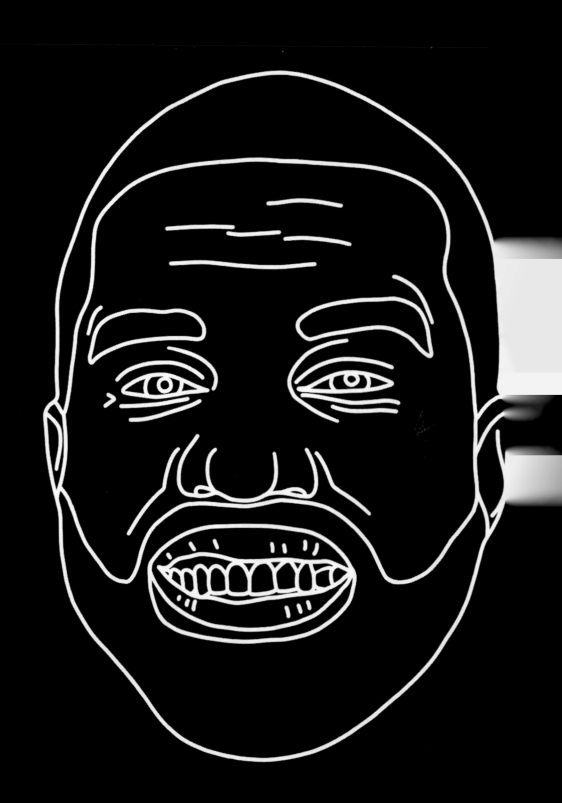

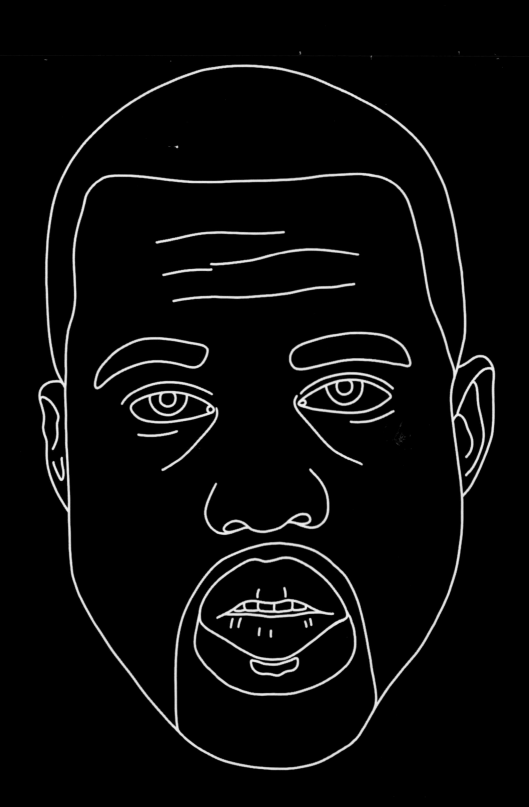

 @kanyewest

You may be talented, but you're not Kanye west

Retweets and comments   Likes

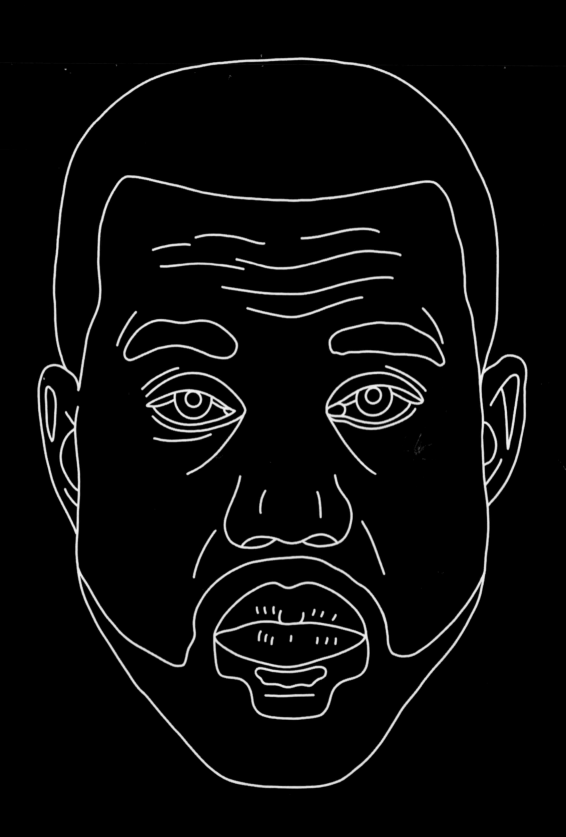

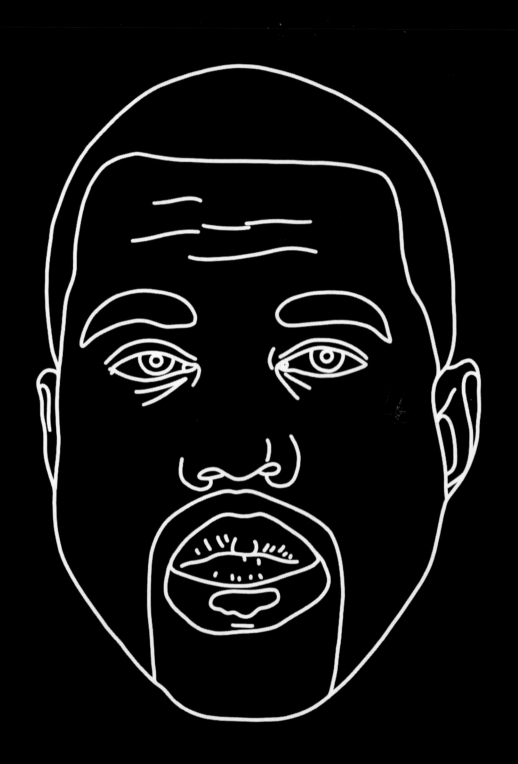

@kanyewest

Is illuminati and devil worshipping like the same thing... do they have a social network that celebs can sign up for?

Retweets and comments   Likes

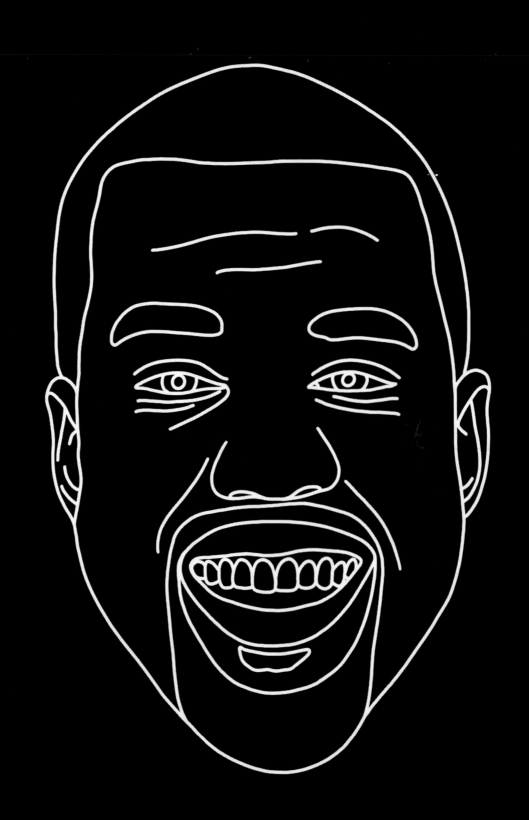

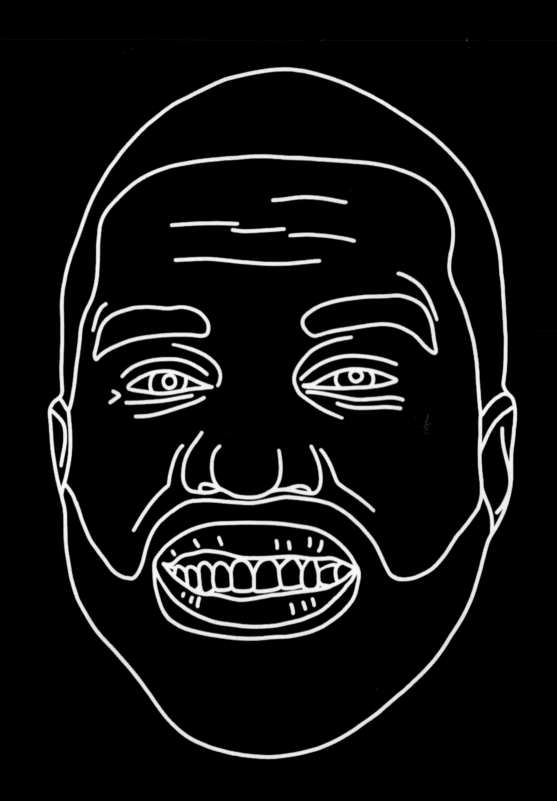

 @kanyewest

You have distracted from my creative process

Retweets and comments   Likes

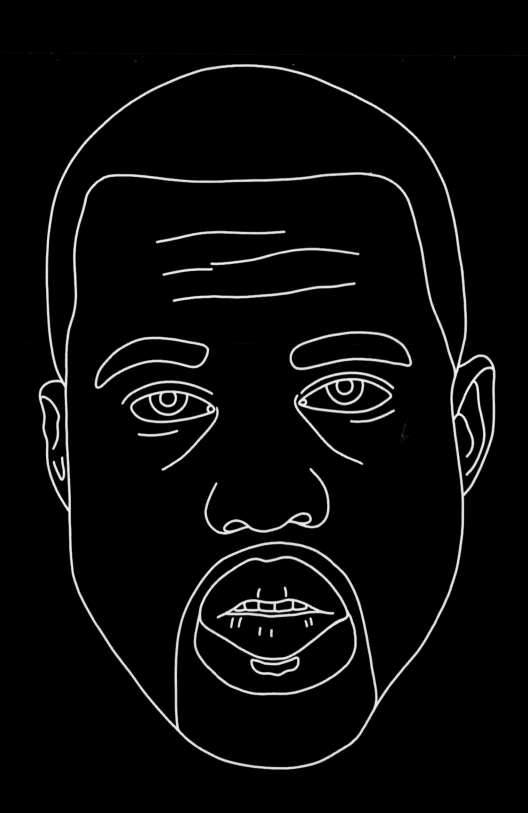

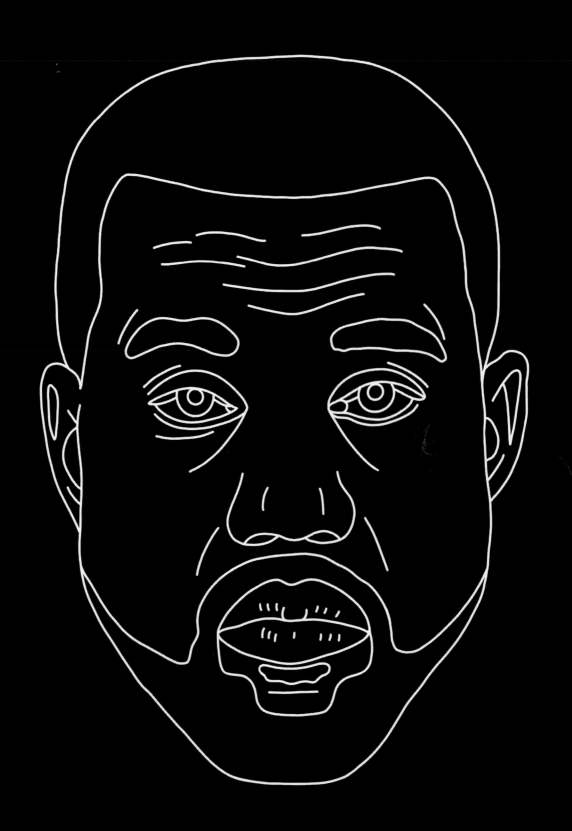

@kanyewest

Maybe I couldn't be skinny or tall but I'll settle for being the greatest artist of all time as a consolation

Retweets and comments   Likes

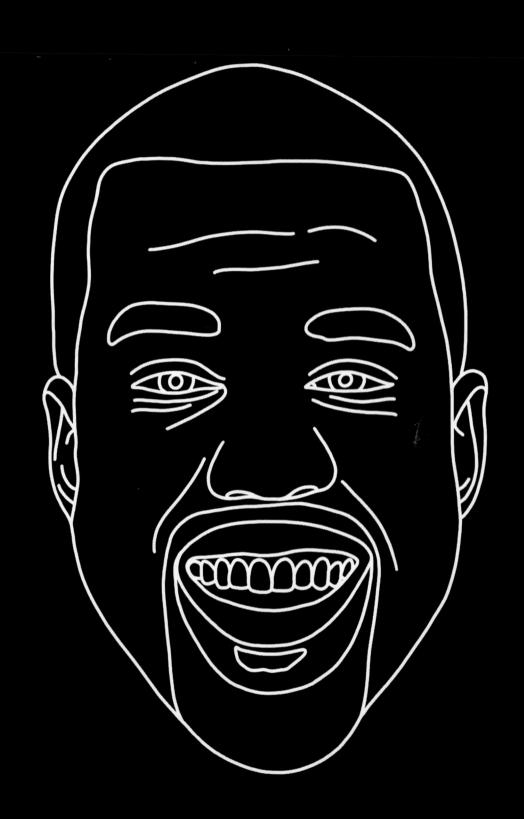

@kanyewest

Floral arrangement is crazy nice right now... these are manifique... I hope that's how it's spelled in France language lol!!!

Retweets and comments   Likes

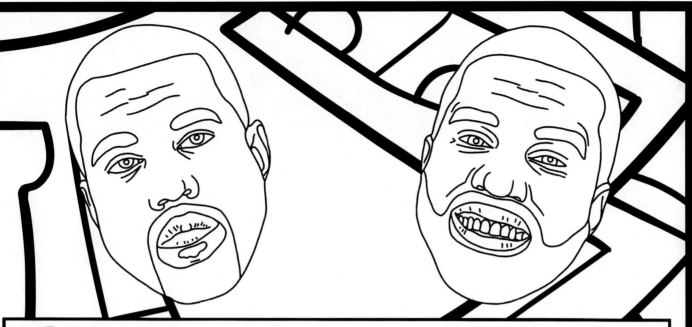

 @kanyewest

I need a room full of mirrors so I can be surrounded by winners.

Retweets and comments   Likes

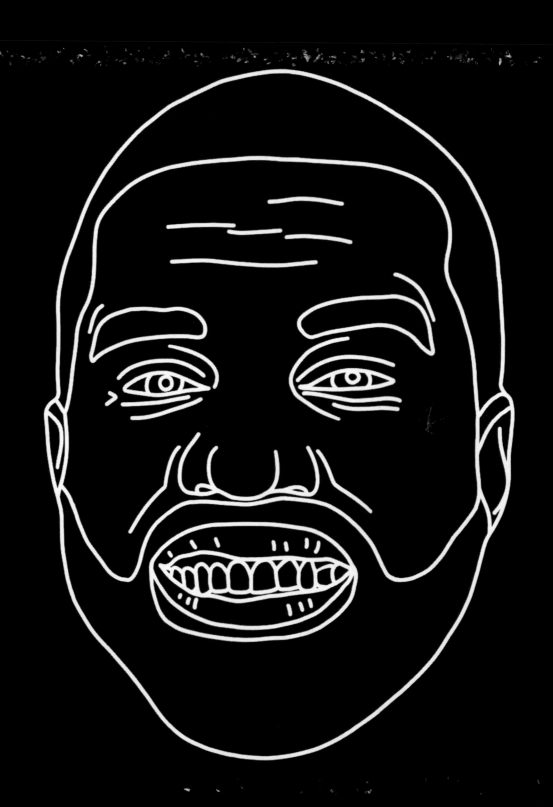

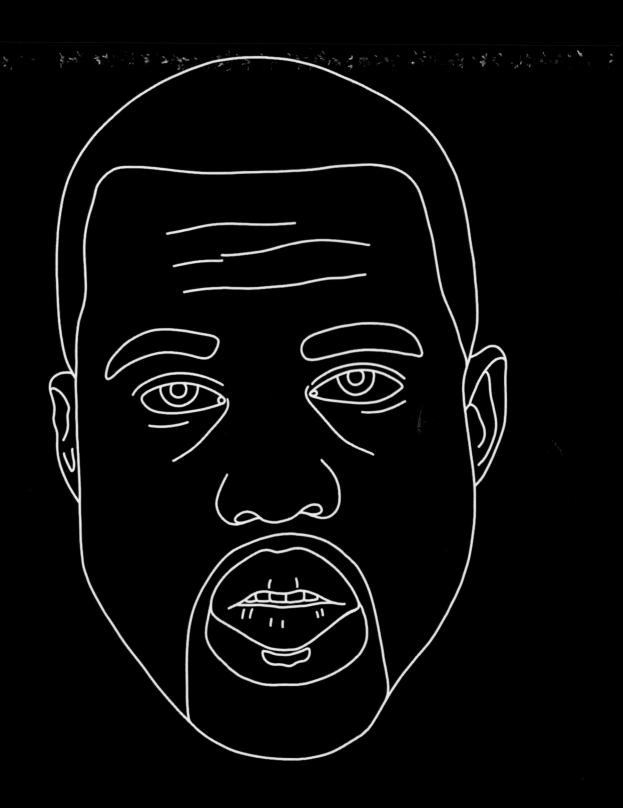

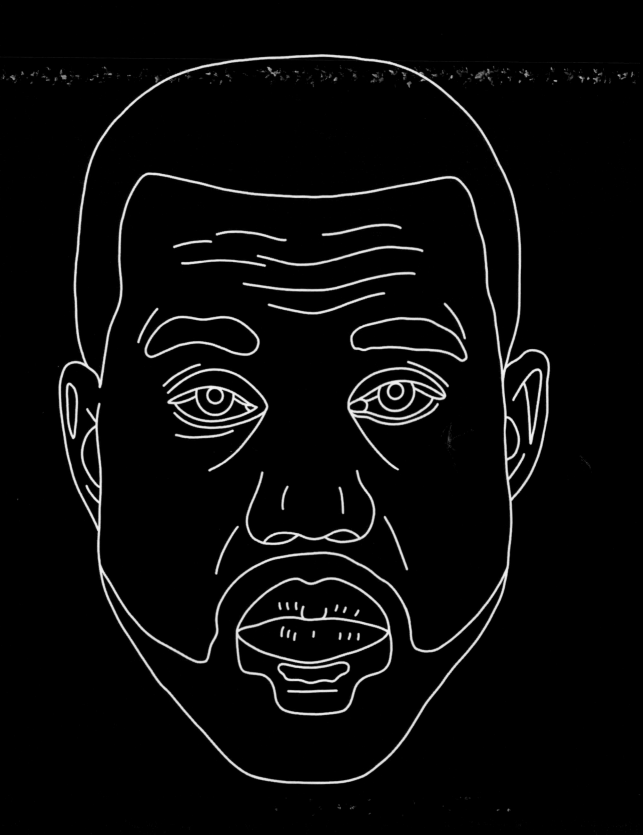

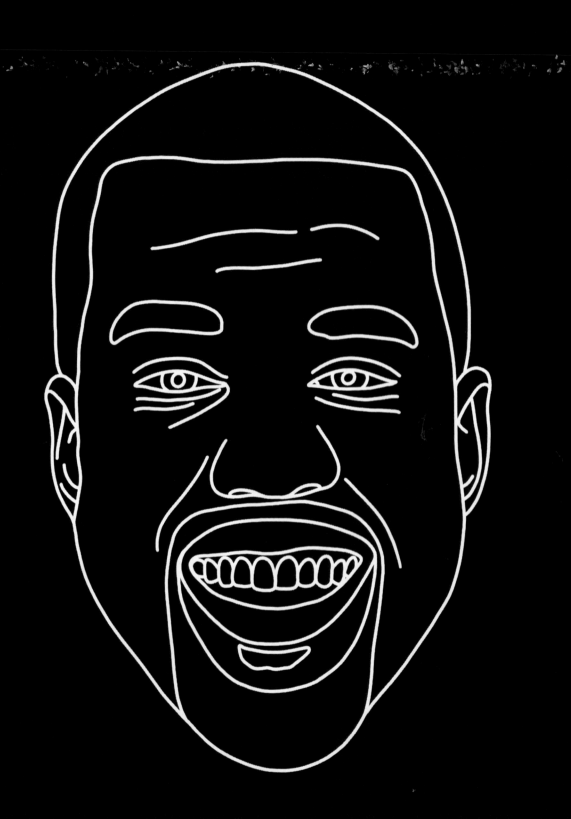

@kanyewest

Room service uuuuugh! I hate when I order fruit and I can taste the other food they cut with the same knife. Beef flavored pineapple

Retweets and comments   Likes

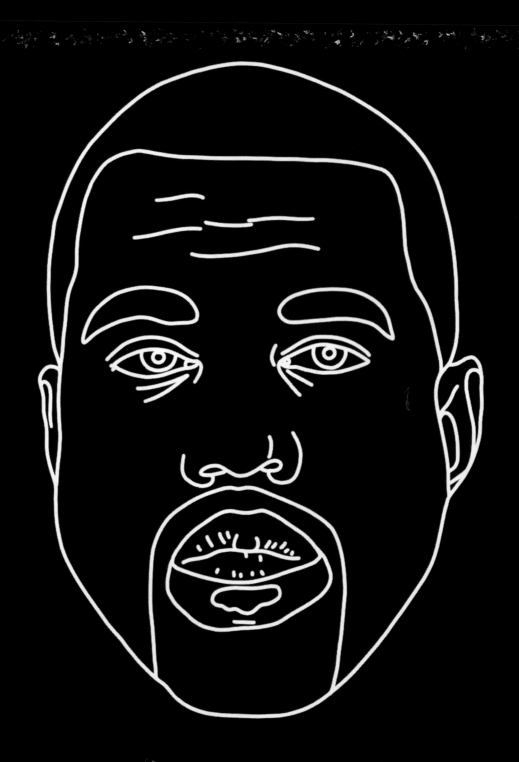

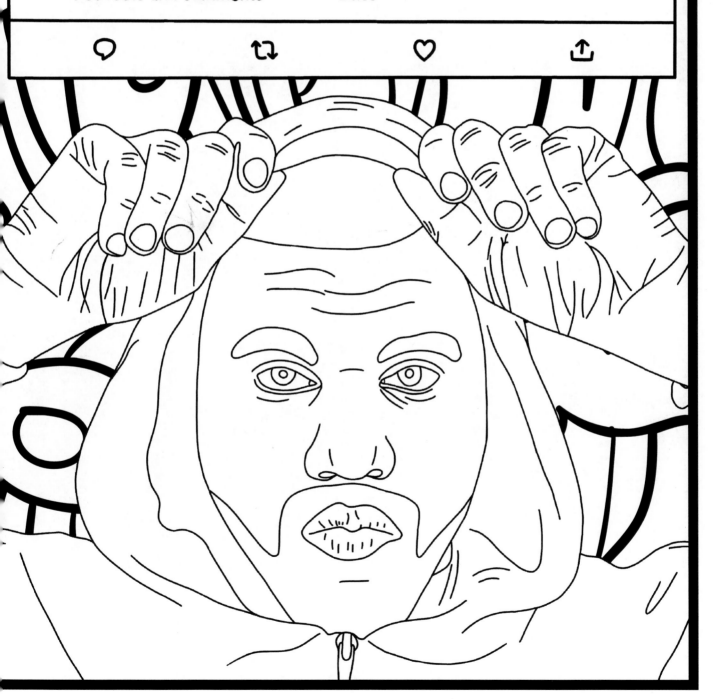

@kanyewest

I understand you don't like me but I need you to understand that I don't care.

Retweets and comments   Likes

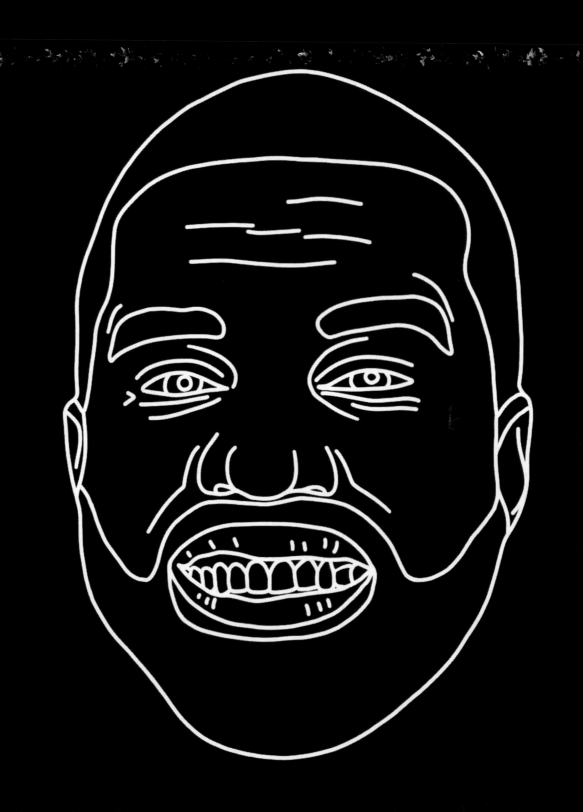

 @kanyewest

Hi Grammys this is the most important living artist talking.

Retweets and comments   Likes

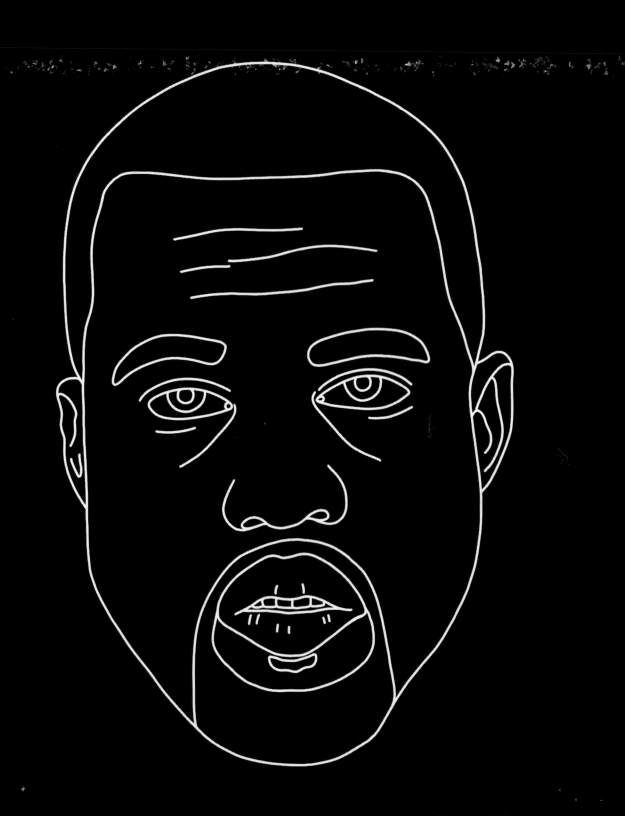

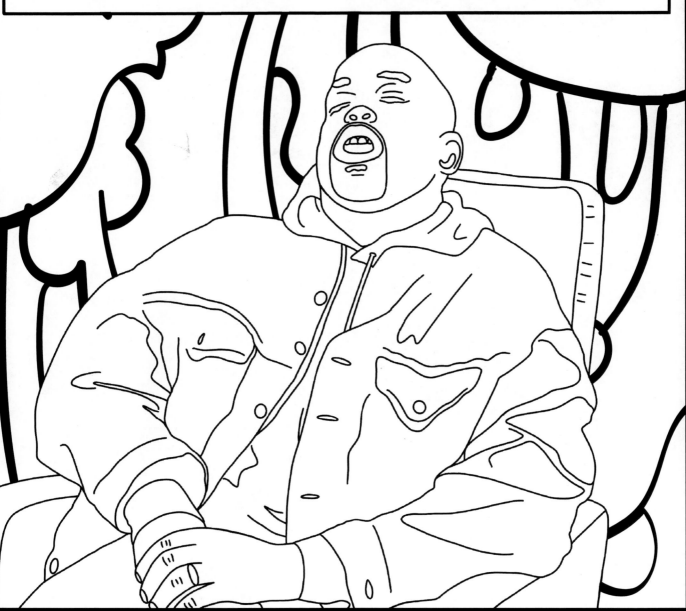

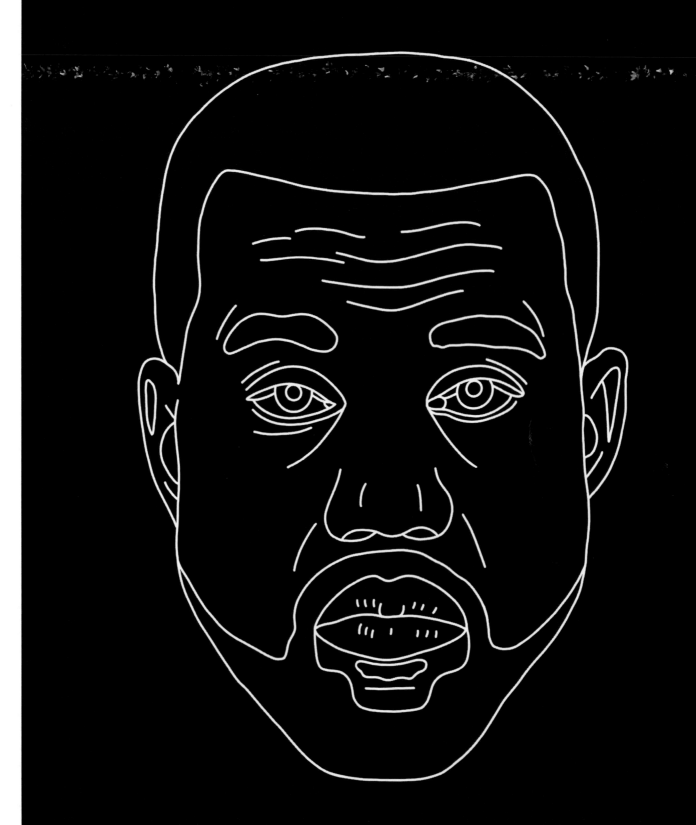

I specifically ordered persian rugs with cherub imagery!!! What do I have to do to get a simple persian rug with cherub imagery uuuugh

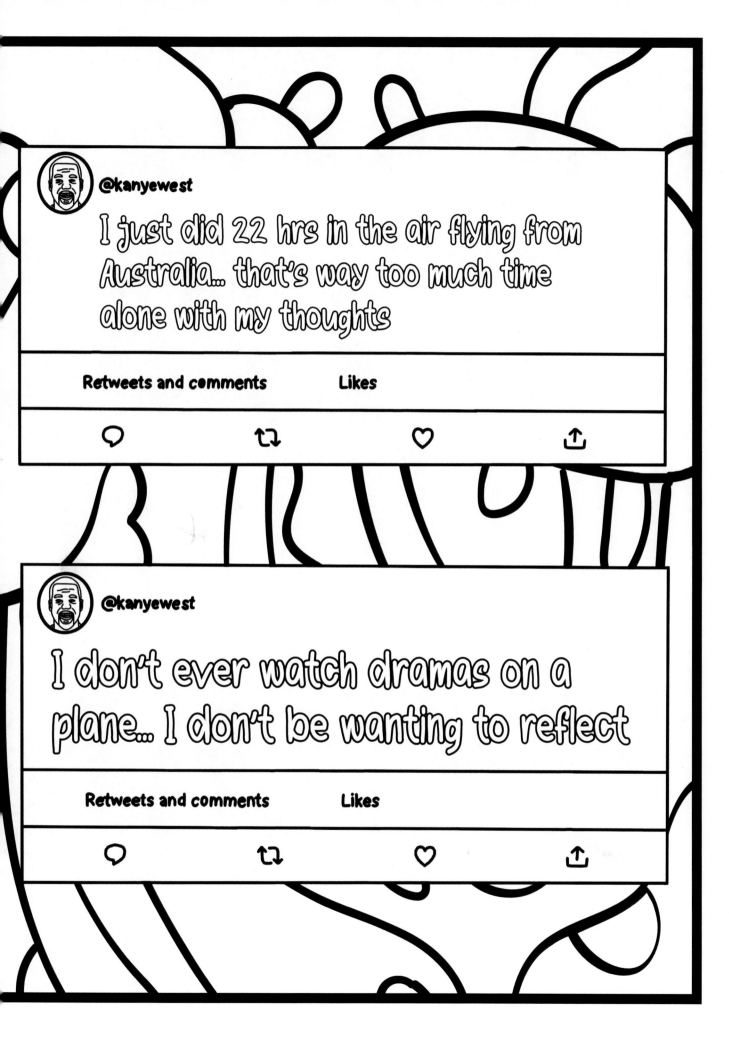

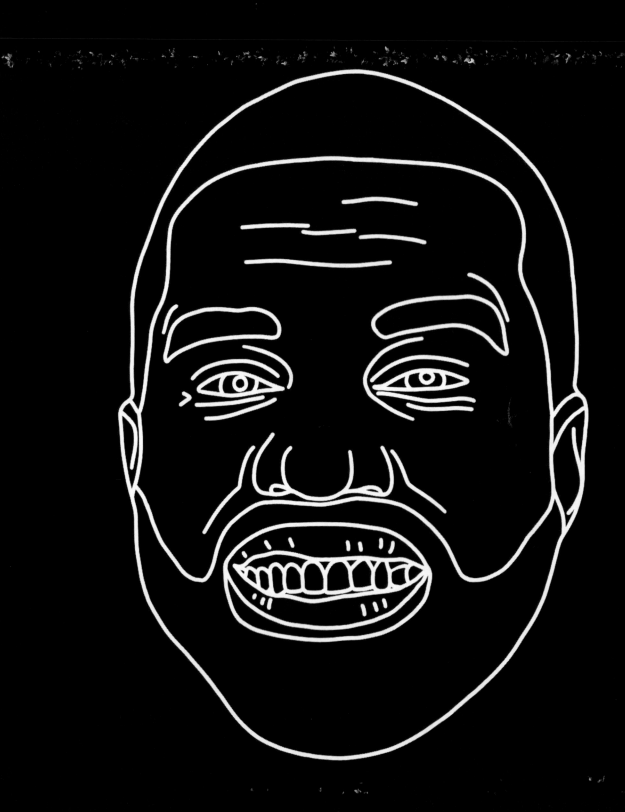

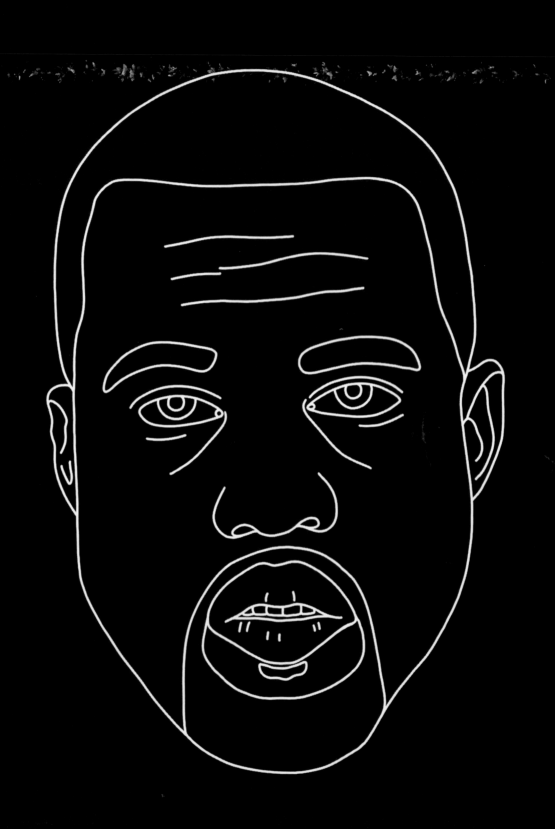

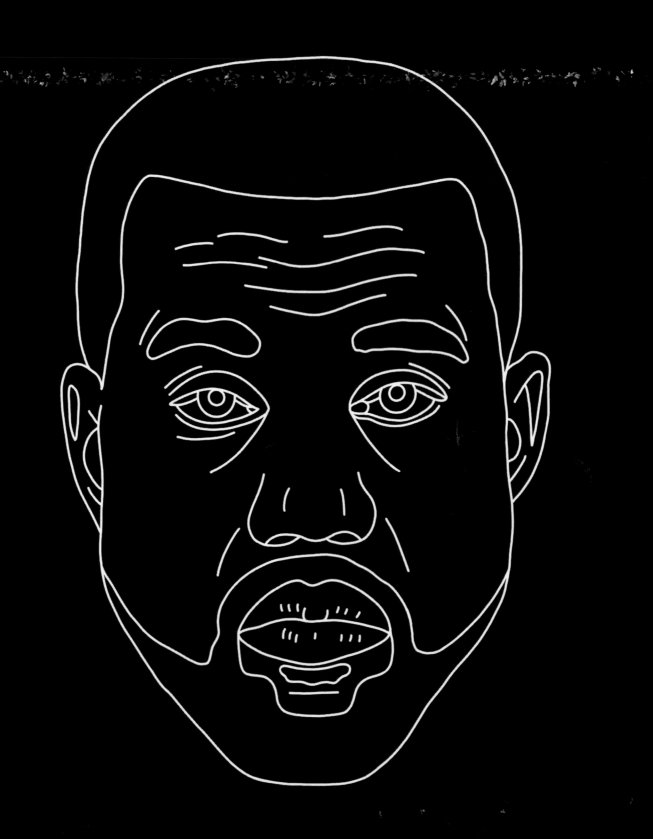

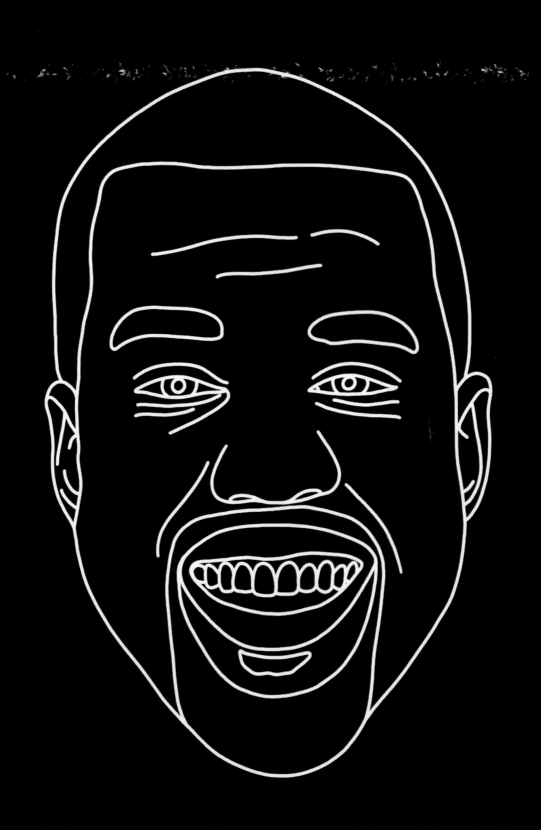

@kanyewest

Do you know where to find marble conference tables? I'm looking to have a conference... not until I get the table though

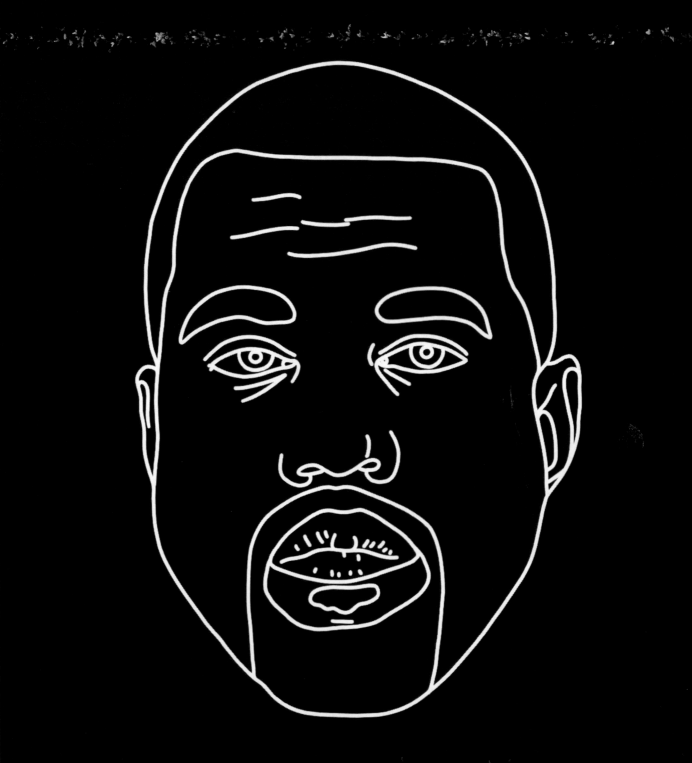

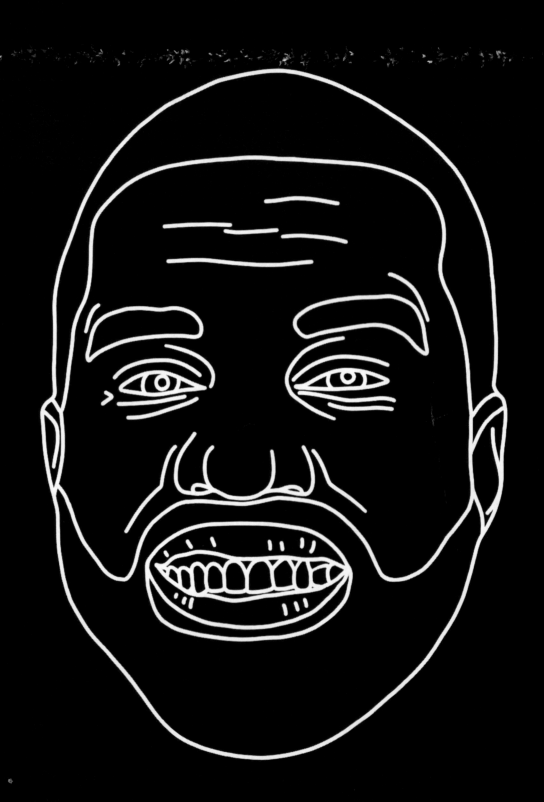

@kanyewest

My favorite unit of measurement is 'a shit load'

Retweets and comments   Likes

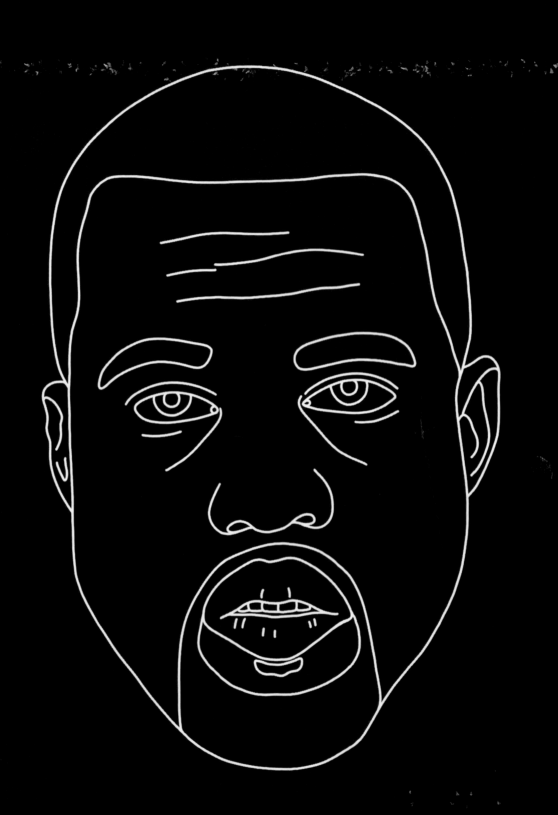

@kanyewest

I think Twitter was designed specifically with me in mind just my humble opinion hahhhahaaahaaa humble hahahahhahaahaaaa.

Retweets and comments   Likes